God Made Me A Perfect Weapon

In His Hands, I Can Kill and
Destroy the Works of the Devil

ATRELLE WEATHERSPOON

ISBN 978-1-7376237-4-8

Atrelle Weatherspoon, ©2022 All rights reserved. No part of this book can be reproduced in any form or by any means without permission from the publisher.

I would like to give a very special thanks to many friends and family for their support in wanting to see this book completed.

My heart goes out to these very special friends
for their help and support:
Pastor Ronnie Whittier
Elder Reddick
Pastor Howard Butler
Mother Barbara Daughterty
My wife, Evangelist Teresa Weatherspoon

Most importantly, I thank Jesus who has always shared with me through dreams and visions, His love for me and all of us.

Thanks to my Lord and Savior Jesus Christ and a very special friend Dr. Wilbert S. Clark, President of the school- Army of the Lord Bible Training Center.

Table of Contents

Chapter 1: Inequities and Separation 1

Chapter 2: Sin Is a Choice 6

Chapter 3: God Knows My Heart 10

Chapter 4: Watch Your Mouth 15

Chapter 5: Sex Sin 19

Chapter 6: Much Fruit 23

Chapter 7: Be a Doer 26

Chapter 8: Bodies a Living Sacrifice 30

Chapter 9: God Will Not Hear Their Cries 34

Chapter 10: When I Can't Find God 38

Chapter 11: To Find God 42

Chapter 12: You Can Lose Your Salvation 46

Chapter 13: To Be Saved 50

Chapter 14: Be You Holy 54

Chapter 15: If You Love God 58

Chapter 16: You Are Perfect 62

Chapter 1

Inequities and Separation

What are iniquities? Can they be unfair behavior? Can it be wickedness of the mind and body, to see the truth and not except it? Can it be to know good and not do it? What about to find out that there is a God and he has been talking all the time to you, but you would not listen to him? Tell me how deep can our iniquities really go to be offered such a great love like this and turn it down? This iniquity will see you real soon. I've learned that our iniquities will catch up with us if we do not turn to God. God really wants to be involved in our lives. God once told me that if I keep on doing what I am doing, I will keep on getting what I am getting. If I change what I am doing I will change what I am getting. Without God, we are trapped in a world without love or hope and where death may come in many unseen ways. Iniquities wants to crowd itself around and in to your life where it can have total control and not God. The key to victory over our iniquities which include hatred and evilness is that one must keep their mind stayed on God. That's right, practice makes perfect. Practice reading the bible and God will stay on your mind. It has a way of getting in to your heart. I've learn that my mind and my heart enjoys the same things in life.

Have you ever read the book of Job? He was a man of exemplary faith blameless and upright. One who feared God and turned away from sin. Oh yeah, it can be done. Even Jesus said if you love me you will keep my commandments. Can you tell me how much you love GOD? My friend, stay in the presence of God and He will build a hedge around your life as well. You know Satan gets discouraged when he can't look over in to your place of drilling. I don't know anyone that would like to have any type of mess track into their home. What makes you think God is going to let that happen in heaven? Our iniquities trouble God and he will separate you from them, or He will separate you from Himself. Iniquities are bad for one's health. They destroy the mind, body and soul of all that will play around with them. Once again, iniquities are sin, and sin does not love you. Sin really is a form of hate acted out towards, God.

You know what else sin is? It is self inflicted nonsense. You know we hurt ourselves and others when we do not follow God perfect laws. Can you tell me of someone you know that has been separated from someone that they loved? Was it because of sin? Satan uses this tool to damn your life. Iniquities destroy marriages, homes businesses, education and jobs. Please don't let sin rule your life. There should be only one King in your life, our Savior Jesus Christ. Don't let Satan subjugate you and lead you into self-pity, addiction, and the many forms of depressions. God told Cain that sin crouches at the door for everyone, but we are to rule over it. Don't let sin separate you from the love of God. My friend, you really are someone to God. Don't let wrong decisions take you from the love of God. Keep God in focus. Fight that devil with all your heart, soul and mind. Do not let anything my friend, separate you from the love of God. Don't you know you're to be firm and to stand strong for God? God will help you to live and walk in obedience to God's perfect will. If you will only follow Jesus Christ, he will lead you to real success. Failure is not an option. Put your trust in God. I will say it once and again to be a conqueror. You must be conqueror first. So why not let God do it for you? Then God will trust you with real authority. Did you know that God is a holy God? To go to heaven, we must be holy also. He that lives after the flesh will die in the flesh. There is nothing that you or I have achieved or accomplished that will go with us in to heaven, but the love and sacrifice of a surrendered heart chosen to be given to God. The fear of separation from God should be so strong in our lives that it become an unconceivable option. For those who are in love with God, remember this. The further away you are from God, the further away you are from great success in the ability to do great works for God. If anyone chooses to be separate from God, they choose to separate themselves from eternal life. So stay connected to our lord Jesus Christ and you will find all things are possible. Life is hard enough. Living against the word of God so why ruin this life and the next one to come. Salvation only comes through Jesus. If you will let Christ live in you then he will make you so complete you will be a new creature and old things will become new. Only the weak will talk about what's in their hearts, but the strong proves what's in their heart by their works and known deeds. Iniquities is the order of death and set back and all of the other horrors that one can imagine. Tell me have you ever thought of the possibility that you might be on your way to hell. Do you belong to a church were the members believe that there is a heaven and hell and where the pastor seeks to see the member growing in God? Can you fill the growth of spiritual maturity in your life?

Many people are standing still. Many people are sitting on the talent that God gave them. That is a sin in God's book. Don't let laziness take the place of been a good and faithful servant. Don't let that be the thing that separated you from the love of God. It is your choice you choose life are death.

Scriptures:

Matthew 12:30, Mathew 25:41, Matthew 25:46, Mark 9:43-49, Luke 13:3, Acts 17:31, Romans 1:24 Romans 6:23, 2 Thessalonians 1: 8-9, Hebrews 9:27, 1 John 2:1

Chapter 2

Sin Is a Choice

For God has given to you and I a great and powerful gift. The gift of choice. Come on, I will explain on the way. Each person born is born in sin and shaped in iniquity. Sounds like there is no hope for us, but that's far from the truth. Especially for those who have chosen to walk in Jesus Christ for they are a new creation in God. Listen, Jesus would not have come if he knew that we had no choice in life. Trust me, Jesus is the best choice that anyone could ever have. Stop! Warning! Caution Be Advised! A note to the reader born in sin and shaped in iniquities. Not anymore.

For those that are born in Christ Jesus is born in a newness of life. No longer or they shaped in iniquities. But in the likeness of their Lord Jesus Christ. For if we will let God write his story on our hearts. Then we will abide in his love. I know that true repentance will put to death sin in our life's. This is truly the best choice that we can make. Hey, you and I know that Satan has a way of deflecting the truth. Satan will flood our mind with so many earthly choices. Thanks God for the help. Do you know the ten commandments? Thou shall not.... Well it works. God helped us in our decision to make wise choices. I have learned the yoke of Jesus is easier and his burden is so much lighter.

Don't let the veil of sin keep you from seeing the love that God has for you. Do you think that making the right choices in what is right and wrong is so hard? Well it can be if you don't have the right type of light on the matter. Do you see now? Jesus are you telling me who you know that is wiser then God? Well then, let God help you with all of your choices and you will have great success. How you live your life should be very important to you. Especially, life after death. Sin is a choice like heaven or hell by pleasing yourself. Are pleasing your creator? It will be too late on judgment day to say, "I wish I could go back and change that". Trust me, sin is no joke and God is not laughing. Sin is like a friend that will always say, "Will you come and die with me?" Yeah, it's like cancer. It chooses you. When you choose to sin, you don't have the right to choose the consequences of those choices. Come on, think about it. Don't let sin take away the beauty of this life and the next one to come. Listen up. You don't have to sin. If you will only choose the life of Jesus Christ, he will able you to triumph over sin. O yeah, in the end we win. Yes, sin is powerful but you have the choice to use a more powerful weapon the love of God. The bible says that in Jesus Christ we can do all things. So let us live in the choices that will defeat sin in our lives. If you will study your bible, you will find that God has given all of us the answers to a good and prosperous life. Sin may get one to the top, but sin won't keep one there. If someone chooses to sin just because they like it, then they have chosen not to be with God. Your sincere love for God will help you to not let sin have a foot hold in your life. Can you believe it? Jesus has given you and I the power to choose Him and the devil can't stop it. Yes, we can have authority over sin. All because of what Jesus did on Calvary. I ask God can I truly live a sinless life? He answered me, "If I live in you and you trust in me, then Satan will have no authority over you." Please do not let anyone trick you into believing that no one can live a holy life for God. For God has chosen you to prove then all wrong. Practice each day the life of Christ. For it has been said practice makes perfect. My friend, you can go to the next level in God and see how great the joy of the lord really is. I've been told that nothing beats a failure but a try. My daddy said to me, "Give it your best shot, son". I bet you won't guess what my mama said to me. Yes, mama said, "Knock him out." "Better Satan than me," my Pastor said. I'm glad that sin is a choice and on one has to go around saying, "The devil made me do it". Isn't God good? He whom the son has set free is free in deed. So think about it. It's your choice.

Scriptures:

Genesis 4:6-7, Deuteronomy 30:19, Joshua 24:15, Psalm.51:1-10 Proverbs 3:1-35, Proverbs 14:12, Ezekial.18-4, Acts 22:16, Romans 5:10, Romans 6:3-4, Romans 6:14, Romans 6:23, 1 Corinthians 10:13, Galatians 6:7-8, Ephesians 2:15, Philippians 4:8, James 1:12-15, 1 Peter 2:21-24

Chapter 3

God Knows My Heart

How many times have you heard this old saying, 'God knows my heart'? It almost makes me want to laugh each time I hear anyone say those words. I have to prepare myself before I can witness to someone because they are going to use this line on me. And yes, I have also said it, too. It's a nice way to tell someone they can't judge you, but thanks to God I now have the opportunity to help others to understand what they are really saying. One thing is true about this saying, God really does know our hearts better than we do. He can see the deeper things and those hidden secrets that lie in our hearts. I've learn that no one knows their heart unless it is shown to them by God. That's right, the word of God is like a mirror. It will show everyone their true nature. God's word will show us the path that we are on and the choices that will come to us. Guess what? The devil knows your heart also and he can't wait to suggest the thing that will damn you, hurt you and separate you from the love of God. How often do you think about your love for Jesus? Or how can I be of help to the kingdom of God? Nevertheless, some will say, "But God knows my heart." The only way people can see your heart is by your works. Look at this, some will say, "I go to work on those days", or "I'll come when I get some church clothes", or "Man, I'm just not ready yet". We say that God know our hearts, but are we trying to know God's heart? Wanting to do something and not doing it won't get you anywhere. Trust me, God is not a fool and we can't fool him. Anything you or I put before God, He is unpleased with it. Somehow we become the judge, jury, and executioner over our lives. We believe that we have the right to tell God why we should go to heaven. Tell me, do you fight sin that tries to enter into your heart? Is there a place in your heart that God has prepared for Himself? Do you spend quality time with God? If not, then you will not have no quality service with Him. For the heart that is in love with God seeks to please the lord. A good heart that is created by God is filled with the beauty of all the past, present and future love that God has done for them. Is this what you see daily in your heart. Or do you have a void in your heart for what God has done and is doing for you. Most of the time we choose to think on the things that will build our kingdom. These choices will entertain us on the best ways of how not to get into heaven. The bible teaches us how to maintain a clean heart. Let the Holy Spirit help you. The world pushes it's way in to your heart. So, let the word of God push it out. Feed yourself with the amazing beauty and truth of a living God. Jesus came to change our heart soul and mind.

Ok, I know what you are thinking. No one is perfect, but if you let Jesus into your heart, He will make you complete. Has it ever been said to you to follow your own heart? Well, we all are accused of doing that and if we are not careful we will do God the same way. We will become so occupied with the thing that God has given to us that He will not be first in our lives anymore. God wants to bless us in so many wonderful ways but we block his line of communication by only hearing what our hearts is looking at. Remember that God is such a perfect gentleman that he will not force His will on anyone. It's not that God doesn't know our hearts, but that we should be learning the heart of God. Tell me, do you know Psalm 1:1? How often do you think about the love of God? Do you have a desire to be in the house of God? Tell me how much time do you give talking with God? To some people God is a perfect stranger. Please don't let that ever become you. God wants to be the perfect friend. Or is that too hard for Him? You know, I found out the hard way that good thoughts don't make good people and not all good people go to heaven. You must be born again. Only true repentance will touch the heart of God and send the help that will start the transformation of a new heart and mind. For as there are master watch builders, God is the master of all the hearts, souls and minds of people everywhere. He and he alone knows your heart. If anyone comes to Jesus and ask help of him he will turn no one away. Yes, Jesus is the master architect and master builder of all that is seen and unseen. Did not he create Adam and Eve? Did he not put flesh on the dry bones in Ezekiel 37:1-14? Then why can't he give you a new heart? Can it be that you love God but you're not in love with God? Can it be that someone or something else has your heart? I've been told that our hearts only have so many beats. How many beats of your heart have you given to God? Can Jesus feel your caressing love when you read about him and his sacrifice for you? Can't you see now? Not only do all good hearts not go to heaven, but those who have those self-made hearts. Jesus said, "There's none good but the Father." My friend, I have prayed that you, too will receive the new heart of God. And that your eyes will see the treasures of God and all the wonder that He has in store for those that are in love with Him. My motto to God is that He did it for me.

So, I will do it for Him. No one can choose this one for you.

Scriptures:

1 Samuel 16:7, Psalm 44:21, Psalm 139:1-4, Psalm139:23-24, Proverbs 21:2, Proverbs 3:5-7, Proverbs 5:12, Proverbs 16 :25, Jeremiah 17:9-10, Matthew 5:8, Matthew 6:21, Matthew 15:18-19, Mark 7:21, Luke 6:45, Luke16:15, Romans 8:27, Ephesians. 6:6-8, Revelations 2:23.

Chapter 4

Watch Your Mouth

How funny can we be with the things that we say? With words, we can make people feel better, give them hope, and make them laugh. Remember, God said let there be light and the light was good. The words that we use mean so much to our creator. Even Satan is listening to our conversations. Did you know that what is in your heart your mouth will speak? The words that we choose to use will indicate how much room Satan has in our heart. Have you ever heard that actions speak louder than words? So, I guess it's safe to say the greater the thoughts the greater the deeds. Good or bad. I once heard it said that the Holy Ghost doesn't cuss, cannot lie, and will do no evil. Do you have the spirit of God living inside of you? If so you will use words of wisdom. Words that will build bridges to friendship. Not words that hurt or push one away. We who are called by God are to build bridges to God. Listen, if any one hurt them with words they will never build that bridge for them. Words can draw or push away. For if we walk in his light, our words will be of light.

What Jesus is trying to get his people to see and to practice is that words make a big difference. As dear children of God, we should meditate often on God and his words. For we have been given great authority to conquer and place sin and Satan under our feet, and words or basically our thoughts into action. The sound of words drives the mind to express what is in one's heart. With Our mouths, we can express how great our love is for God. Angry words can and do fool many people into believing they have personal power. Do you know that every idle word that proceed out of our mouths we will have to give an account for in the day of judgment? I've been told the best way to destroy an enemy is to make a friend of them. How many times have you heard someone's mouth get them in to trouble?

God has said that man shall not live by bread alone but by every word that proceeds out of the mouth of God. Do you believe that God will place his words in your mouth? He wants you to speak life in to other people's lives. People will find it hard to hear you if we let them see and hear Satan in us also. I heard a person say to their friend once that if you can't say something nice about a person, just don't say anything at all. Look, if Jesus showed up everywhere you are, how would you talk? What would your conversation be like? Would he be proud of your language? You say you believe in God, but yet you honor him not in words or deeds. Yes, it's easy to say things we don't mean. With God's help he can help you with your communication. Your yay will be yay and your nay will be nay.

God has given to you and all his children the power to change the world with His words. Will you choose to walk in obedience that gives authority? To those who have faith and trust in God Almighty, words give life or they give death. How will you choose? How you choose to express your love for God will determine how much in love we are with our creator. If our minds are wrapped around God, how better can we please Him today. I believe that God will give to us the things to say to anyone that is asking for a better understanding to life and all its trials. Today, I hear too many people saying, "Man I almost dropped my religion". Sin is not committed only with our hands, but in our minds, and with our words also. Please don't let Satan use or have access to your mouth to kill, steal and destroy future believers. I also believe that we should watch even our expressions on how we talk to others. I've learned that using wisdom and love will help draw even angry and mad people closer to seeing your viewpoint. Cursing and using bad language is just as wrong. Especially when it is coming from some one that has confessed to being filled with the Holy Spirit. Our mouths came make us are break us. For what is in the heart the mouth will speak. Our mouth will show if we stand for God or against him. Let us remember that we are to always share the amazing word of God and as I have learned in some case, I can show you better than I can tell you. I love the choice that I have made to serving God.

Scriptures:

Joel 27:4, Psalm 19 :14, Psalm 29: 1-2, Psalm 34:13, Psalm 37: 30-32, Psalm 139:4, Psalm 141:3-4, Proverbs 8:21, Proverbs 12:17-19, Proverbs 15:8, Proverbs 17:7, 27-28, Proverbs 21:23, Proverbs 31:26, Matthew 10:16, Matthew 12:34-37, 1 Corinthians 15:33-34, Ephesians 4:29-32, Ephesians 5:4, Colossians 3:17, Colossians 4:6, Thessalonians 5:21-22, Titus 3:1-2, James 3:10-18, Peter 1:15-16, 2 Peter 2:11-12.

Chapter 5

Sex Sin

Oh my, yes, He wants me to say something about this, too. Sex is way more than a hyped up feeling. It is a life force that can be placed on speed. Let me make this easy for the both of us. Let's call this word, "it." Ok? It will come right up and into your personal space without knocking or asking for your permission. It will never ask if it is ok to just show up. It feels its in its own right because it is the Queen of Lust. Its desire is to make and have slaves out of all who will drink from its cup of wine. It has been said that its most favorite pets are dogs of all types. If anyone will lend themselves to it. It will give them dreams and visions to become like it. It says to itself, "This is my life and body. I will do as I please". Do you know someone that has said that? I have said it to at one time. Its power is given to it by its lover, Satan and it enjoys killing people and their kingdoms. It destroys families and homes. It'll pass out diseases like it was candy. Its lustful ways have consumed the hearts and souls of all people. Its desire is not to have just you, but to have your children as well. This is an easy task for it since we will not teach our children the laws of God and its lustful ways. Parents, please live the life of Christ in front of your children so they have the will to believe in the words of God. We can prove to our children that our love for God is as real as His love is for us.

There are so many people that will not come to God because they feel they need sex in their lives. Trust me, if we take the gifts of God and make them first in our lives, it will be the gifts of God that will whoop us. This is the perfect place that Satan would like to see you and I in. Do you know that it is a beasts- a common animal? It will try to change your very nature. Things that are good if placed in Satan hands, can be tools for Satan to destroy our lives. Only God can change one's heart, soul and mind. Have you heard of someone that has received an STD that's sexually – transmitted- diseases. It is given to mother's baby without them ever knowing their fathers.

God gave us laws so that we can have a good and healthy life. The act of disobedience to the word of God makes changes in our lives. Sin just don't hurt the one that is doing it, but our sin can hurt many people, friends love one even though we don't know. I've learn that what make you laugh can all so make you cry. If the people we have in our lives is not from God. They will always try to be first in your heart. Don't let easy come easy go take the place of the best thing that has ever happen to you. Hay don' t learn it the hard way. Disobedience to God is like withdrawing your favors and blessing from heaven before you really need them. Did you. Did you know that a real man would love to marry a virgin? The same with a woman. I believe that we can honor God with our mind soul and body. You know He knew you before He created you in your mother's womb.

I've learn that our God is an all some God and he has made a way for all who love him to escape. His terrible wrath that will fall on those who don't love him. This you can believe. God's wish is for all of his children to grow strong and beautiful in holiness. When a person will seek after God, he or she will become one of his most beautiful of creations. When a person chooses to really repent, Satan loses his hold on them. Especially in the area of that strong hold in their life. The fights now become the Lord's fight. My friend, have you ever heard it said, "Just stand there and look pretty?" God wants to prove to you just how much he is willing to make good changes in our lives. God will forgive you even for the worst of sex sin in your life. The Lord is able to take even the power of lust out of your heart mind and soul. He will give to you the joy of a clean heart and life. You will become the person that he wants you to be. Let us all remember that God created us in his image. So please let us walk in that image and not bring on shame to His Holy name. My friend, the power of doing good works lies in the choices that you will make. Either you will serve yourself, man, or God. No one can serve two masters. Jesus told me the flesh is like a dog. If you don't watch it, it will jump up on you and soil your clothes.

My friend it is up to you if you want to live an ordinary life, but if you give it to God, He will give to you an extraordinary life for others to see. What a choice this one is.

Scriptures:

Exodus 20:14, 22:19, Leviticus 20: 15-23, Proverbs 6: 32, Matthew 5 :27-28, 15 :19, Mark 7:21, Romans 1:24-28, 1Corinthians 6: 9, 10: 8, 6: 13-20, Galatians 5 :19, Ephesians 5:3-4, 1Thesselonians 4:3-5, Hebrews 13;4-5, 1 Peter 2: 11, Jude 1:7-8

Chapter 6

Much Fruit

Hey riddle me this. What do you call a Christian that has more fruit then he can eat, that he can store a way, that he can give away? Now, before you look further, try to see if you can answer the riddle. Did you say rich or successful? How about lucky, fruitful, or advantageous. Ok I gave you a hint. He is a man who does not walk in the counsel of the ungodly, he will not only have success, but he will have great success. My Pastor says that a lot. The word 'blessed' in the Greek is to be happy. What I've learn in all my trials is that I had favor in God. I was satisfied with all that he has done for me. My answer to the riddle is, he is satisfied and blessed. The book of Job brings to my mind how Job pleased God and that God placed a hedge around about Job to protect him from Satan. My friend, God has asked all of us to bear for him much fruit. For God is not slack in his promise to show us his great love. Just ask Job. If you really want to be a Christian or have already given your life to Jesus Christ, the Lord himself will place the seed of fruit bearing in your heart. The good thing about this is they don't have to be planted ever again. For the word of God will grow in them that truly love him. Not all words can offer eternal life, but obedience to God offers you more opportunities to be fruitful in the kingdom of God.

Have you ever tried to grow any vegetables that would not grow right and did not taste good? Did you know that there or some Christian just like that? You see our works will come and go, but only what you do for Christ will last. To me, it is a sin to try to go to heaven alone. I once heard it said more fruit, more money, less fruit, less money. So shall it be in the Kingdom of Heaven. Our good words in faith shows our love for God. Jesus said every branch that does not bear fruit in him, the father will cut them off. Please do not hide the talents that god has given to you but use them to do the will of God. Do you not know the beauty that lies in the fruit that God wants to grow in each person that receives the spirit of God? They become helpers to God in his garden. As we strive to become more like Jesus Christ, the more others will see the beauty that God has place in our lives. Please remember that the life of the fruit is not yours, but the word of God place in you. If you ever separate yourself from the love of God, you will become fruitless-tasteless and rotten in the eyes of God. It is true all living things will eventually die. Even the works of our hands will be demolished, but the good things that we have done for God will live on forever in heaven. My beloved friend, become that tree that is planted by the rivers of living waters. For I will always pray that you and I will forever give to others the fruit of everlasting life. Choose the fruit that gives eternal life.

Scriptures:

Jeremiah 17:9-10, Matthews 3:10, Matthews 7:16-12, Matthews 12:33, Luke 3:8-9 Luke 6:43, John 15:1-8, John 15:16, 2 Corinthians 9:6-7, Galatians 5:22-2, Ephesians 5:9-11, Colossians. 1:10, James 3:17-18, 1 John 3:9

Chapter 7

Be a Doer

I believe that you have heard this old saying before, "What have you done or what have you done for me?" Ok how about this one, "Where were you when I needed you? Do you know that everything that we say or do is being recorded and written down? No one will be able to lie or deceive the King of Kings. Each day we wake up, Jesus is given us a chance to live the best life that we could offer to him. One day Jesus will ask you, "What have you done with the time I have lent to you?" Will you be able to say, "I spent it with you, Lord?" This I have found is so very true that when I become active in God's word, all things fell in place in my life. Oh yes, the more I do the more I want to do. I have found that there is a special joy when I am doing something for the Lord or being obedient to my Lord. God has proven to me that if I participate in the works of God, He will participate in the things that will bring us joy and great success. It's been said that no one wants a slacker working for them. They just can't be relied on. If your works are for yourself, then you would have laid no treasures in the kingdom of heaven. Truly where our treasures are there is where our hearts are. The thing that we love, we will be found doing them. Tell me, do you love God and are you in love with Him? I know a man that loves his wife and she loves him also, but they are not in love with each other. That kind of love will not go the farthest for it is not complete love. I've learned one thing that we will be doing, and that is the thing that we love so much. My friend, where is Jesus really at when it comes to what's first in your heart? We work very, very hard to build up our 401K and a pension just to put something away for a good retirement, but most of us don't think much about life after death. God is busy with all of his creation, but most of all with your and my life. I thank Jesus Christ for not letting us die. His grace stayed with us till we learn just how great his love is for us. Tell me, how much time do you give to God each day? Do you even ask God what can you do to show your love to Him? I bet if you read your bible more you will find the will of God tailor made just for you. Oh yeah, God has laws and we must be found doing them. If you love me, keep my commandments. Jesus said you'll know if anyone is truly born again because they live in the word of God and His words live in them. Listen to me, if you have no works in God then you do not have His spirit living on the inside and you are not hi child. It is very possible to put stuff and things first in our life and make God second. Please understand, God must be first. When you do the will of God, He will bless you to overcome bad habits to grow in faith and to have tranquility and insight in everyday life. The beauty of being a doer will keep you in the presence of God. Did you know that while you were being a doer for God, He was doing the thing that was greatly blessing your life? God has shown me that it is better to give than to receive. Each time I share the love of God with my neighbors, I feel the eyes of Jesus looking at me. I have found that it is hard for me to explain this unspeakable joy I receive in doing his will. To be a part in helping others to find God. O yes I have learned that this is one of the ways for a born again person to see the Holy Spirit working in people's lives. The more you become involved in God's plan of salvation, the better you become knowledgeable of how God is working to make you a better warrior in his kingdom. You and I know that we can't do more for God than he can do for us. My question to you is, why aren't we doing all that we can to prove just how much our love is for him? To love God is to love his word and to love his word is to live in His word. To live in his word is to be found doing his word. It is not what a man says that defines him, but the works of God in his life that he lives openly. One day we will all stand before the great white throne judgment of God and He will ask you, "Show me your works." To be asked, "What have you done for my father? Who will come and share with me the love you shared with my Father? Which one of your enemies will say to me, "My lord, he showed me your light and lead me out of the darkness into your marvelous light?" Let it not be said that you gained the whole world and lost your soul. To be or not to be God's doer. That's your choice.

Scriptures:

Proverbs 6:6-9, Proverbs 10: 4, Proverbs 20:4, Matthew 7:24, Luke 6: 46, 8: 21, 12:43, John 8:47, Romans 2: 13, 8: 9, 12: 1-2, 1 Corinthians 15:58, 2 Corinthians 5:10, Galatians 6: 7-10, Philippians 3:14, Colossians 3:23-24, Titus 1: 16, James 1: 22, 2:14-20-26

Chapter 8

Bodies a Living Sacrifice

To some people this title may sound a little weird, but don't you know everyone has sacrificed something in their life at one time? Have you ever given up something that you really wanted so that you could gain something better? Some people call that trading up. Tell me something, have you ever took something that was yours and gave it to help someone else? How good did it make you feel Did you know that each time you gave up something that you needed to help others, you were putting up treasures in heaven? Hmm, that's being a sacrifice. We can learn how to please God through self- sacrificing. Remember Jesus Christ was our sacrifice. He gave up his life so that you and I can live. How much time should you are I offer to Jesus each day?

How much of your heart is Jesus holding in his hand? Do you even know where God is right now? I've learned that if I only do the thing that I love, then there is no offered sacrifice. Tell me how would you fill if you found out that your parents never went out of their way to be a help to you? If you know to do good and fail to do them, you sin and that pleases the devil. I know no one wants to give up the things that they have. Oh, but I have learned that God always gives better. It's like given up something old and with little value. Compared to what Jesus has for them that are in love with him. Did you know that God wants more than the things that he gave to you to enjoy? God wants to be loved by you. We must keep our hearts and our minds ready to do the will of our lord and savior. Trust me if you call yourself a Christian or a child of God. Your faith will be tested to prove to you just how much you really love the Lord. Do you know that our trails come to show the areas that we need help in. The love that we say we have for God should immediately make changes in our lifestyle. This is the type of sacrifices that God is looking for. When we learn to fight Satan and not the ones God is using to strength us we grow in God. When you live a sacrificial life in the name of Jesus Christ. We show that the spirit of Christ does live in us. There are so many things that we can do wrong with our lives, but we must remember that we are no longer our own. You have been brought with a price. A marvelous life and a new creature are you. So tell me then how can you step out of the word of God and do what you like? To me that is going back into sin. Either you will live holy or not. We must allow the Holy Spirit to lead and guide us in all righteousness. This is where the real sacrifice comes in. To be are not to be. To choose in your heart that you will be unique in the hands of God. Please my friend, don't let anyone convince you that you can't live a holy lifestyle for God. God said all things are possible especially to them that believe. Listen, you can live the life of Christ you talk about. I was told that Jesus was God in the flesh. Is that not all so true with you and I? God in us.

In order to live a sacrificial life, we must devote much time in prayer and fasting and the reading of the word of God. Always remember that someone is looking and listen to who you say what you are. Let not your good work be evil spoken of. Did you know that our body language and facial expressions can lift one or send one away? I know that God can put a joy in your heart that will be prefect in all situations. Don't you know that God is the one in total control? So, let him have your life then you can cast all of your cares on him. So you must believe and except that Jesus Christ is the sacrificial name of God. He gave of himself and His life so that you and many shall have a good and bountiful life now and in the kingdom to come. Have you ever heard it said that the needs of the many outweigh the needs of the one? Well, God really proved his love to me. For God so love the world that he gave his only begotten son. That whosoever believeth in him should not perish, but have eternal life, (John 3:16). Are you a person of conscious? Will you take the love offered from someone and fill you and owe nothing to them in return? They that live with honor will show the laws of honor in their life. I have an old saying, If he did it for me I will do it for Him. Can you say that? Jesus is the perfect sacrifice for you and I. Can you find in your heart enough love to return to God a life full of sacrifice that will give him the honor and the glory that is His? Really it's a good choice.

Scriptures:

Psalm 51, Matthew 25:21, Romans 8: 9, Romans 12:1-21, 1 Corinthians 6:15-20, 2 Corinthians 5:17, 2 Corinthians 5:15, Colossians 3:22-25, 1 Peter 2:11-12

Chapter 9

God Will Not Hear Their Cries

It's hard not to hear someone crying. Especially when they are very close to you. Today we can see so much pain and hurt that is in our world. I think that we both can agree that there is no shortage in our trials and tribulations. All over the world, sin is on an up rise. Can you remember some one that has brought tear to your eyes? You know most of the troubles and pain that we receive in our lives can be said that we did them to ourselves. Come on, think about it. Have you ever heard this saying, "Ok, keep it up" or, "Don't do that" or "Didn't I tell you to stop?" I believe you get the point. See, someone was trying to save you from some type of trouble. Sometimes, pain can be our best teacher. A true fool is someone who will keep on trying to do something that will not work the way they want it to go. Our Lord is trying to keep us from making bad decisions that might end our lives or extend our pain. No one knows the time that their grace will run out.

Don't be like the boy that kept crying wolf- a Christian now and in a few minutes, something else. You see, God knows our hearts. He knows who is real or not. When I was young I remember making promises to God that I did not keep. I felt ashamed and told God that I was sorry, but I kept doing them over and over again until he filled me with the Holy Spirit. Is there someone you know that makes it very hard for you to believe in them? Sin has consequences and you won't get to choose the punishment. My pastor always says that. Most of the time people will not speak to God unless they need something from him. Do you know when God is talking to you? Can you feel his presence before he speaks to you? Have you ever become tired of talking to someone that will not even try what you are asking of them to do and you knew that it would bless them? Soon you will just stop trying and let them learn it the hard way. Well, God will let one choose for themselves also. The love of God has made a way for us to escape much of our pain and suffering. I've heard of others who have asked God for many things and did not receive them. Why should God do for you what you can do for yourselves? I've learned that God does help those who need him. Have you tried to return that love to God? How many times have you turn away from his laws. How many times have you had the opportunity to do good and make God proud of you and you turn him down? Remember this, God doesn't owe us anything. If we think of all that he has done for us when we were living in sin, we might have a change of mind and heart. How many times have you heard it said, "I'm not ready for all that?" How faithful has God been to all of us? Can we truly get mad at God if he doesn't answer our prayers? Wow, and we continue to do as we please with our lives. It is God's love that is trying to keep us from pain and disasters that waits for us all and the biggest one of them all is eternal death. That is hell my friend and some people don't believe in that place, but me, myself, and I are not going to take that chance. Jesus said if you love him to keep His commandments and I believe that Jesus will help us to do just that. Do you want God to answer your prayers? He will if you ask him with a sincere and truthful heart, but if we don't talk to him and listen to him when he calls, why should he listen to us when we call on him? God does hear all of us, but he knows our heart's desire and if we will listen to him. God knows what we need in our lives and when we need them. When we ask of anything from God we should say, "If it be thy will Oh, Lord" because if we put anything before God and his will for us, it will be that thing that will whip us and terrorize our lives. Tell me, if God hears sinner's speeches then how much more will he hear of them that love him and keep his commandments? Don't just call on God only when you need something, but build a relationship with Jesus Christ so you will know that it is He that is speaking to you and no one else. If you answer His call, he will answer your calls. My friend, seek the Lord and learn his voice. You will be amazed at what he will show and tell you. Take time and let the lord know how you feel about him. Give to him the quality time and the quality service that he deserves. If we could only see how much the Lord our God loves us, we would become so overwhelmed with joy and living a holy life to prove how thankful we are to have Jesus in our lives. I have no complaints. Still having trouble with that choice.

Scriptures:

Deuteronomy 1: 45, 2 Samuel 22:42, Job 35:12-13, Psalm 18: 41, Psalm 34: 14-17, Psalm 66:18-20, Proverbs 1: 27-31, Proverbs 21 :12-13, Proverbs, 15: 29, Proverbs 28:9, Isaiah 1: 15, Isaiah 59:1-3, Jeremiah 14: 11-12, Lamentations 3:8, Lamentations 3: 44, Ezekiel 20:3, Hosea 5:6, Micah 3:4, Zechariah 11:13, John 9 :31, 2 Timothy 2 :12, Hebrews 4 :14-16, James 1:6-8, James 4 :1-4, 1 Peter 3 :12

Chapter 10

When I Can't Find God

Boy, have you got a big problem if you can't find God. You are not looking in the right places. You know he's not hiding. He loves you too much for that. Tell me, are you hiding something from God? Can it be sin? What about the lifestyle He desires for you to walk in? Many people ask themselves, "Why am I here?" The truth is to have a blessed life. The kind you can only have with Christ Jesus living on the inside. I've learn something about people most of the time we do it to ourselves. There is something in each of our lives that encourages us to say to ourselves, 'I did it my way'. We bring on most of the trouble and pain that we receive in our own lives. We know that pain is the hard way to learn what not to do, but a true fool is someone who will keep on trying even when they see it just won't work. God who loves us so much is trying to give us time to see that He knows what will work in that special life that he gave you and I. My friend, no one can find God if all they want is to not go to hell. God knows your heart and our desires. Do you want him or what he can do for you? I've learn that if you look for God you will find him. We must get involved with the things that God is involved in then we will find that we walk in His salvation. Did you know there is a book out on how to find God? It's called the bible. If we seek him with the whole heart, faith will open the doors of the eyes, the mind of the soul, and the new life that God has in store for those that love him. If one gets real with how they really want to live their lives with God. They will see the joy of the Lord. Did you know that Jesus has wrapped his grace around all of us until we could see all the opportunities that he has given to all people? Make time for God and you will find he has always been close to you. The truth to the whole matter is how much do you love God? Jesus said, " If you love me you will keep my commandments." Each time you say no to sin, the more of Christ Jesus you will see and the more authority you will have over sin. That will show the more of God's love that is in you. Usually when a person wishes to obtain an item that they want, they go where it can be found. Have you tried asking an anointed man of God? Sat in a prayer group? Have you tried true repentance? How about trusting in the word of God. If anyone chooses to walk in sin they cannot have a good relationship with God. We should not focus on the things of this world, but on the things that Jesus spoke of in the bible. We must understand that sin doesn't want you to find God. Sin will always point one in the wrong direction. So we must not take our heart soul and mind off of the things of God. It is very hard to see God if we are looking at other things. Many people will tell you that they have God living on the inside, but they fail to live a holy lifestyle. If one will give to God quality time and quality service, God will implant his richness into that person's life. I have found that when I say no to myself and do it the way he asked me, I receive great joy from my actions. The more we live in the act of obedience. The more of God we will see of him. God will act and participate in our lives proving that he is with us. No one will be able to accuse God of hidden form them. If anyone truly want to find God. They must deny themselves first. I've learn that God is a perfect gentleman. He will leave it up to you to accept his plan of salvation. Are you read to let Jesus be your Lord and Savior? Are you ready to give God your heart soul and mind? To place God's values over your personal desire, have you made up your mind to live like a true child of God? Joining a church won't bring God any closer to you. If someone wants a closer walk with God, they must study to show themselves approved unto God. Learning and seeking what his will is for you will place you in the heart of God. One can't lose if they're that close to God. So I'll ask you, are you man or woman enough to try to go to the next level in your life. Jesus is waiting to offer you a new life; one with promise hope and power. Remember this, you don't have to find God. Just get on the king's highway. He will take it from there. Be real with yourself. Are you truly wanting a closer walk with God? My friend, let Jesus Christ fill you with his spirit and you shall be made holy and walk in the newness of a new life. I can't choose nothing better than that. No one born comes in looking for God, but Jesus knows when we become sick and tired of being sick and tired with our lives, then he will come and offer us a new life. Are you ready to choose now?

Scriptures:

Hosea 4:6, Matthew 6:33, Matthew 7:14, Matthew 1:14-15, John.10: 25-28, John 12:38-40, Romans 128-32, Romans 8:7-8, Romans 10:17, 1 Corinthians 11:18-21, 2 Corinthians 4:3-4, 2 Timothy 4:3-4, 2 Peter 3:3, 1 John:11, Jude 1:18-21

Chapter 11

To Find God

Have you ever wanted something so bad that you could have jest tasted it? Ok, I don't know about you, but I thought I was just going to lose my mind if I did not get the thing that I wanted. Many of those things did not do what I thought they would do for me. We all seek after stuff and things we think will bring us joy. Many times we learn that those things that will make us laugh, can make us cry, but the gifts that God wants to bring into our lives will bring great and eternal joy.

This is what we learn as we walk with our savior Jesus Christ- He knows the desires of our hearts better than our wants. Many people choose not to believe in any GOD if they can't see or hear or make him perform in a manner that they like, but they forget one thing- that God knows the intentions of our hearts. My friend God is not lost and neither can we lose him. Look around and see what God has made. God is not dead, He's still alive. You ask me how I know. That's a perfect question! When I got sick and tired of being sick and tired of how my life was going I let faith do its job, and boy it came in like a mighty rushing wind. He told me everything I needed to do to see and to hear him, even how to inherit eternal life. My friend, never give up hope in God. Go to your bible and read it. Listen to the people in the bible and how the spirit of God moved upon them and how the Lord used them to do great and mighty things. A wise man told me once, if you want to find someone, go to where they hang out. Stand where they play. Learn what they like. Soon they will come to you. Do not get mad at God if he doesn't come right away. Remember you weren't looking for him at one time. There is a way to get God's attention. Go to God with honesty in your hear, have faith that he will hear you, and then find a good church where the heart of the pastor is in God's hands. Seek God to be filled with his love. That is, the Holy Spirit for God is love. Seek him with all of your heart, soul, and mind and he will lead you in the path of his righteousness. The beauty of God's love to us is more then we can imagine. Can you imagine all the grains of sand that is on the earth and that He loves us more then all of that? Just look at the nail prints in his hands and feet. God is not hiding from us, but sin will make the Lord hide his face from us. God made salvation very easy and yet most people make it hard. Many claim it's too hard to understand or it's too hard to live. The road to salvation does not start with us and it will not end with us. My friend, the only way to get into heaven is by our Lord Jesus Christ. There is no other way. You cannot bypass Jesus and go directly to God the father. Jesus died at cavalry on the cross for the sins of the world. Make very sure that you understand this and serve the right God for we all will live in eternity somewhere. So, we all have a choice to make and just to let you know, yes, life has been better for me since I gave my life to Jesus. Now there is a joy that lives in me and each day I enjoy getting up just to share God's love with all living things. If you really want to find God, then repent of all your sins. Be honest with God and He will hear you. You know as well as I know life is too short to play around with it. It goes as fast as it came, but God will help you make the best of it all. God told me that if I keep doing the thing that I am doing, then I will keep getting the same results. Change what I do. I will change the results. If we don't change our life to include God in it, He will not be in it. My friend, always include God in your plans and you will have great success. For God will open up the windows of heaven for you. That's not too hard of a choice is it?

Scriptures:

Psalm 14:2, Psalm 32:6, Psalm 63:1, Proverbs 8: 17, Proverbs 8:35 Matthew 6: 33, Matthew 7: 7-8, Matthew 10:39-40, Luke.11:9-10, John. 4:23, Acts 17:27 2 Corinthians 5: 17, Ephesians 1: 4, 2 Timothy 3: 16, Hebrews 11: 6

Chapter 12

You Can Lose Your Salvation

You know, I believe that everyone has a story that they could tell somebody about something or someone that meant so much to them. Some things or so precious that they hurt us very much if we were to lose them. Sometimes we are able to get over them or just replace them. Our salvation should mean so much to us that we will not allow anything to take its place or remove Jesus from our lives.

Most people don't believe that they can lose their salvation. It takes more than works to please God. Within every one's heart, there lies a treasure that everyone will seek. If that treasure is not to have faith in God's word, one will not please God for it takes faith to bring about true repentance. Others believe that they have to keep on repenting, and yet I know some people who love Jesus Christ so much that sin can never be an option or a choice. I've learn that when a person stays away from God and His church when there is no prayer or witnessing going on in that person's life, they might allow Satan to take the place of the Holy Spirit in their lives. Sometimes that person cannot recover. Many has gambled on, "I'll make this my last time." In doing that it costs them more than it was worth. My friend, what profits a man if he gains the whole world and loose his soul? Someone please tell me why do so many people want the things that this world has to offer. More than the treasures that God has to give to those who live in obedience in him. Did you know that you are to become a new creation while you live on this earth? A person that can defy the laws of man and nature in Christ Jesus only. That person will never say the devil made me do it. There are so many that believe that they can try to reason with God on why they had to do what they did, but God's word is final. Who wants to play with that? Some others think that good thoughts make good people. No so can an atheist that do good things have no faith in God, die and go to heaven? No. The same will goes for them that will not seek him or seek the indwelling of the Holy Spirit. I've heard some say God is too good to send people to hell. Other say but he said that if I ask Him to forgive me, He will. People seem to forget that God cannot be fooled. It is the devil that has many people fooled about the love that they have for Jesus Christ. There are far too many people that do not consider God or think of him in a day or how his words can bless them within that day. So many wake up each day and leave this life without God's salvation. Do not believe that you cannot lose your salvation. When you forsake the will of God and do it as they say- 'I did it my way', then you reject God's only way and that way is only through his son, Jesus Christ. Many people can feel that wonderful change that they had with Jesus slipping away, and that strong will to be close to him and do whatever their hands can find to do for Him. My friend, be strong in Christ be who you are supposed to be, dear children of the most, high God where in you all things become new and old thing pass away. Do not give up and always seek God's will and let the word of God led you by His Spirit. Satan will try over and over to remove you and to turn you and your heart away from God. Keep telling yourself, 'I have the power for all that live in Jesus have been given authority and power over sin and darkness.' My pastor, Ronnie Whittier always tells us that you can choose to sin, but you can't choose the consequences of your sins. Look, if you are really real with your salvation, there is no power on earth or in heaven that can take away our salvation. So keep your faith and stay on course. Choosing God can never be wrong and if loving Jesus is wrong, then I don't want to be right.

Scriptures:

Luke1 2:46, 13:6-9, John 6:66, 15:1-6, Romans, 11:20-22 1 Corinthians 9:27, 2 Corinthians 5:17-18, 1Timothy 4:1, Hebrews 3:12-14, 6:4-6, 10:25- 26 2 Peter 2:20-21, 3:17-18, Revelations 3:5, Revelations 22:19

Chapter 13

To Be Saved

Hello, can you hear me now? All righty then. It is a proven fact that most people do not know what to do to obtain salvation. Many others are not sure if they are ready to give their lives to Christ. Many others are not serious enough to live the life of a warrior for God. Look, the work of salvation has already been done in and by Jesus Christ. Every person has been given the opportunity to receive the gift of eternal life. There is a way to know them that are saved among us for they live in faith. In their hearts you will see the life of true repentance. Obedience to the word of God is their only lifestyle. You may say that is impossible, but to God all things are possible to them that believe. Hello, are you still there? Do you want to be saved? Ask God with sincere love in your heart. Be sure you want to commit to giving Him your life. Trust in Jesus Christ with all that you have, then go and be baptized in the name of Jesus Christ for the remission of your sins then seek the Lord to fill you with His Spirit. We sometimes call it the Holy Ghost. Then you will have the authority of God to place sin under your feet. If we live our lives in Christ Jesu, we will not fulfill the lust of the flesh. One thing is for sure, if a person is not focused, he might have a hard time completing their mission. I believe that anyone that wants to go to heaven should make that trip their top priority. Many believe that once saved always saved, but your name can be blotted out of the book of life. Many will say I haven't done that much wrong for God to put me in hell. Others will say, 'But I attend church and paid my tithes.' All these thing are good, but verily I say to you that good people will go to hell. It's not about being good. It's about been born again. Living a new life that is not of this world, allowing the Holy Spirit to help us make the decisions that God has given to us. For whosoever will place their faith, heart, love, and obedience in the hands of God. For the Lord redeems the soul of his servants and none of them that trust in him shall be desolate. Learn of him and let this mind be in you that was also in Christ Jesus. Remember that sin is death and will keep on asking all of us will you come and die with me? Know that God has set us free. So live free in the power and the authority of his righteousness. Always remembering that Satan is defeated by our Savior and Lord if we who are called by His name and Live in his perfect will, the Lord will help them to become his champions. It is God that gives us the desires to seek Him. He creates these strong desires in our hearts that helps us to want to become a chosen weapon in His hands. To be saved is very simple. Choose you this day to serve the Lord. Live your life to the glory of the Almighty God so that others may know that you are a child of God. Let the people see God when they see you. Let them hear God when they hear you. Always remember you can show them better than you can tell them. Always push yourself to read the Word, to study it and to share it and never stop seeking to stay busy in God's kingdom. It will promote the proper attitude in wanting to remain a born-again believer. I believe that anyone that desires to be saved should be just as strong as their desire to hear God say, "Well done my good and faithful servant."

Do you want to be saved? Do you know what Jesus Christ is requiring of you and I who say I love you Lord? We are to love the Lord with all our heart, and with all our mind, and to love our neighbor as thyself. Have you ever thought of the possibility that if you give your life to God, you might be the one who brings many souls to the Lord? To be are not to be, that is the question spoken by Prince Hamlet. I also like the song that Isaac Hayes sang, 'If Loving You Is Wrong, I Don't Want To Be Right.' You see, that's the way I feel about Jesus. I like that type of a choice. Salvation over Hell, that sounds so good to me. Now that's what really rings my bell.

Scriptures:

Isaiah 45:22, Jeremiah 29:11, Luke 13:3, John 1:12, 3:16, 10:9, 6:40, Act 2:21, 2:38, 4:10-12 Romans 6:23, 10:9-10, 2 Corinthians 7:10, Eph. 2:8-9, Titus 3:5, James 1:21-23, 1 John 1:7, 5:3-4, 5:12

Chapter 14

Be You Holy

Yeah man, you heard it right, and I do believe it was said by God. Look, unclean people cannot enter the kingdom of heaven. Frankly, I don't blame Him. I once brought home a stray dog that had fleas. Trust me, I will never do that again. I have a friend that took a trip and brought back bed bugs. You know, he is still trying to get rid of them. God is not going to make that mistake. He will separate us from sin though the power of the cross. You see, God created everything and out of all of this, He made us special. We are to be separate so that we can be given a very special and unique love. One that will promote His people to give to Him an unwavering, unstoppable love that will last forever. It is God that sets us apart so that we can become a very special gift to others. He takes us from being ordinary to extraordinary people. The Lord has gifted His people to be able to do His most perfect and wonderful will. I don't know about some folks, but I love what he has done with my life. I had too much of me, myself and I. Too much of this, that, and the other to even enjoy myself or get ahead in life. Many people don't even know what the word Holy means or represents. To those who truly walk with Jesus Christ, they know that they have been set apart and are separated from the things of this world and the evil to come. They desire to be dedicated to God. My friend, it takes God to give us these strong desires. If we love Him and make Him first, our heart will flourish in wanting to be holy. God is holy and the angels at his throne cry, "Holy, holy, holy is the LORD of host." Isn't it beautiful that our Lord and Savior wants to make us and take us to a place where we will live with him forever in the beauty of holiness? I believe the children of God can tell them that labor among them. There is a gentleness that is loaded with wisdom and of words that speak life to all that they encounter. Haven't we all heard this old saying, "Practice what you preach." I've wonder is this one of the reasons why many Christians will not speak of the goodness of God. Can this be why sin is on the rise in our homes and communities? When do we decide enough is enough and holiness is the standard that God requires that we have in our lives? Shall we continue in sin and saying to ourselves, 'But God knows my heart?' When do we become children that are strong soldiers for our Lord and Savior? We can't do this of ourselves, but if we believe the way we should, love Him the way we should, study Jesus the way we should, then the beauty of holiness will cover us as the air we breathe. If you think the earth is a beautiful place now, wait until he redoes it and puts a new you in it. I believe that throughout time there has been others that have loved God as Job loved God. All of us have choices that we will have to make as a Christian and that is how close we will walk with the son of God. How much of your best will you give to God? Believe me, it is not impossible. God wants us to have that kind of a drive in our lives for him. One in which God requires that we do justly and to love kindness and mercy and to humble ourselves before God. If God requires this, then I know it can be done. I have never felt this way before. I thought I was enjoying my life back then. Now I see the difference in living for me and living for Christ Jesus. For me and my life, I will never leave home without Him. Having the Holy Spirit in my life is the best thing that has ever happened to me. I can only imagine where I would be now if I had not decided to walk in the path that my Lord and Savior has laid out for me. We must be brave and prove to all that see us or hear us that there has been a wonderful change that has come over all of them that believe in Jesus Christ. If our Lord said, "Be ye holy for I am holy," that should be good enough. When a Christian seeks to please the Lord our God, he walks in the atmosphere of the favor of the, all powerful God. Do you seek to please the Lord? Then let him do the things that he has created for your life and the beauty of holiness will forever be in your life. Yes, in Christ Jesus we become awesome. I am glad that he chose me. Aren't you?

Scriptures:

Exodus 22:31, 30:29, Leviticus. 10:10-11, 11:44-45, 19:2 20:7 20:26, Numbers 15:40, 2 Kings 4:9, Mark 1:8, Luke 1:70, Romans 14: 17, 1 Corinthians. 6: 19, 2 Cor. 13:12, Ephesians 1:4, 1Thessalonians 5:27, 2 Timothy 1:14, 2 Peter 1:15-16, Peter 1:21, 3:11, Jude 1:20, Rev 20:6, Rev. 22:11

Chapter 15

If You Love God

How many times have you heard this said, "I love the Lord?" Really, love is not a strange word. We use this word to express the way we feel about the things we have in our lives. Who can say how long these feeling will last? I know people who say all the time, "I love the Lord," and will not go to church. It sounds like an old saying to me- I love my job it's just the people that I hate. Can we as people truly know what is real love? It took the bible to show me. I've learned a true saying in life, that which we love can make us cry. Have you ever heard someone say this, "I love him but I'm not in love with him?" Can there be any truth in this? I think so. I believe it to be true. Look at how we treat one another and the ones we say we love.

Can there be any power in love? Can love truly change one's life? Can love change all things? I know so. I believe that true love, that's the real stuff that comes from the heart of GOD. My friend, do you truly know him? Jesus said if you love me keep my commandments. Now, tell me now how much you love him? People always tell me no one is perfect or that Satan is a powerful adversary. These words only tell me just how much you know of the bible and about the love you know of the one and true God. I believe love can move mountains. Each time I think of how Jesus carried my sickness and problem on his shoulders, I then become stronger. I now know that if I owe anyone anything in this life, I know for sure I owe Jesus Christ. I now see that it was Him that took my lick. He became bruised for my iniquities. He accepted my death sentence and he wore my death shroud. Truly it is hard for me to believe that many people are not in love with Him for that reason alone. When I look back in to my past, I can see that if it had not been for God in my life, it would be very unpleasant now. Does the love that you say you have for God bring glory to His name? Do you delight yourself in the beauty of his love? Can you feel his presence? When he comes close, I've learned that those that are in love with God, they run to win. They are excited about the things that God has done in their life and the joys that they know that are to come. It is so hard to explain the types of joys and beauty that is in the hearts of them that is in love with Jesus. He enables us to be more than a conqueror. It is He who has pulled us through. Who can see this without true repentance?

Christ is waiting. How long will you put off not knowing the love of God? Many people love the things that God has given them more than the giver which is God. We give these gift more quality time and quality service than we give God. Many will say that God is first in their lives, but the proof is in the putting. When people see you mimic Christ, they see God. When they hear you speak of the cross, they hear God in you. The awesomeness of our God will show in the lives of those that are in love with God. Can I say this, good people don't go to heaven, only those who are born again. Born in Jesus Christ. The resurrection is for them that walk in the newness of His life. Have you heard it said that with the rich man, money is on his mind and his mind is on his money? That's the way we are to walk with God. If we keep Him in our minds and in our heart, we will find it hard to sin against God. I am always asked this question by people, "Why do you talk so much about God?" My answer to them is, "He's talking to me all the time." They that love the Lord shall be filled with His Spirit. That love shall continually increase as they walk with the Lord. If one is truly in love with God, there is a strong zeal in them to live holy. Have you chosen yet?

Scriptures:

Deuteronomy 10: 12-13-16-19, Deuteronomy 11:1, Matthew 6:24, Matthew 19:16-19-22, Matthew 22: 37-39, Matthew 28:20, Mark 12: 31, Luke 6: 31, 6:37, John 13:37-38, John 14: 15-21-24, John 15:9-13, Romans 13: 10, 1 Corinthians 13: 4-8, Ephesians 4:1-2, Ephesians 5:25, Ephesians 6: 1-3, Peter 1: 14-15, 1 John 1:5-6, 1 John 2:3-6, 1 John 3: 16-18, 1 John 4:7-8, 1 John 5:1-5, 2 John 1: 6- 9, Revelation 14: 12.

Chapter 16

You Are Perfect

Yeah, kind of hard to believe, I too, did not believe in that one. Not until one night in my bed room when I was studying my bible and praying, I ask God to show me something new in His word and boy he did. My jaw nearly hit the floor. You should have seen the look on my face when God said me, "Servant in my eyes you are perfect." No, Lord no one is perfect but you God and Jesus. Again, I heard Jesus say to me, "I love you so much." Then, I jumped up off of my bed and I ran room to room to room looking to see who could be in the home with me. You see, no one was there at home with me at that time. I just knew someone had to be playing a trick on me, but on one was there. So, I went back to my bedroom. Again, the Lord spoke to me saying, "My son, I love you so much. In my eyes you are perfect. Go and tell them all how much I love them. Tell them in my eyes, they are perfect." No matter how much I debated with that thought, I could not get what Jesus had said to me out of my mind and heart. Each page I turn in the bible, I found it was true. God was opening my eyes. In him alone can I be made complete. Have you ever heard it said He's making diamond out of us? Who can really say how the lord sees each one of us? I became very happy when I saw how He felt about me. I said to myself, 'Man I don't know any one that thinks of me like that.' What Jesus saw in me made me wanting to live in the lifestyle He sees in me, and that makes me feel good. Knowing that God loves me that much, I know that in Him, I can do all things that is pleasing in His eyesight. Man has given us many laws, but the yoke of Jesus is easy and His burden is light. If a rich man chooses to move into a broken down home, what do you think he will do to it first. Yes, he will fix it up. If we will allow God into our lives, He will send His carpenter son into our lives. The rich man will build that home into his heart's desire. How so will God create in you the life of His son. Once again, we can't do this, but it is God who makes us the overcomer. We in him become complete. Like the little Choo, Choo Train said, "I think I can. I think I can." Well He did.

God Made Me A Perfect Weapon

Do you believe what Jesus has done is worth a try to practice obedience for the one who gave you and I everything He had, even His life? The little Choo, Choo tried and he succeeded. I was told that practice makes perfect. We know Jesus is perfect and God, well, we have no words to express how great and powerful and glorious He is and with all that perfection living in us. One can't help but to choose to try and want to live holy for the God we love. If one is truly filled with the holy spirit, they are motivated and driven both by God and the love they have for Jesus Christ. Many people will say, "I love God," but they are not in love with God. I believe that God chooses the ones he knows will allow themselves to be fashion into his perfect will. They will allow the lord to conquer all of them and then he will create in them a new heart and fashion them to be the perfect weapon in His hands. The Lord will use them to steal, kill and destroy the works of the devil. Have you not heard it said that the rich man mind is on his money and his money is on his mind? If we keep the love and laws of God which is perfect in our hearts, we to became rich in the favors and gifts and abilities that God alone can give us. My Pastor, Ronnie Whittier always says you can have success, but with God you can have great success. Yes, we all were born in sin and shaped in iniquity. Thanks be to God we can all say not anymore for those who have accepted Jesus Christ our only Savior. Has been born again and given a new life and have been shaped in the image of God's wonderful son. All we have to do is love the Lord enough so that He will mold us into his perfect will. My God knows the heart of those that are willing to live an extreme an extraordinary life for him. I believe that God will give each Christian the opportunity to go as far in righteousness. As their love is for him, each one of us can become a weapon of mass destruction in the hands of God. If our hearts remain in His hands. I believe the reason that so many people fail and turn from God is because they never got filled with the Holy Spirit. Believe me, the Lord will never lose His children. Once you receive His Spirit, it's hard to walk away from that kind of love. The ability to sin will never leave us, but the spirit of God will help us to have no appetite for sin. If you and I will stay focused on the love that God has for us and to seek His will each day, then God will open the eyes of our heart and mind. We become free to wreak havoc on the kingdom of Satan. We can't lose with the stuff God has given us, His only begotten son. Are we just Christians that tries to live our lives just being good? That is not acceptable. Our lord is looking to build Christian soldiers. The ones that He can use to bring many souls into his kingdom. The ones that will go through trials and tribulations to present their bodies a living sacrifice, holy an acceptable unto God. My friend, let God transform your life in to the perfect replica of his son, Jesus so that you and I in His hands can become his perfect weapon. Jesus wants us to live our lives so others will want to be made in the image of Jesus Christ. Don't let the word perfect trip you up. We use that word all the time as in, he played a perfect game, and man that was perfect, or that is a perfect time. How about she drew a perfect circle? Thanks, that was perfect. He has a perfect set of teeth. I believe that Adam was perfect when God created him, but he had a choice to make-The same cohoice that was given to him is also given to us. The choice of life or death. When we decide to live our lives outside the will of our creator. Then we choose to live a life of in perfect ways. Adam dropped the ball and it was passed onto you and I. Will anyone of us fail God as Adam did? The bible shows us that Jesus intercepted that fumble. We have a new coach and owner. Seeing now how great of a love that the father has for us. Seeing now how he alone can repair the brooking pieces of our lives and unite us back into his life making us one with Him again. My friend, because God told me that in his eyes he sees you and I as a perfect child, try not to get hung up on what our Lord and Savior see us as. He showed me that when we get to heaven we will no longer live in our old bodies. God will give us all new bodies. Because of God's grace and merciful kindness toward us, God has proving His love was greater than all our sin. I believe that God saw all that we could become if we would let go and let God have our lives, then we become more beautiful to Him. Can you see now when we get to heaven, we became perfected perfectness? Let us become that perfect weapon for God seeks all of His children to be in His hands. S. K. D. the works of Satan. TIME NOW TO CHOOSE LIFE OR DEATH.

Scriptures:

Genesis 6:9, Genesis 17:1, Deuteronomy 18:13, 2 Samuel 22:31-33, 1 Kings 8:61, 2 Kings 20:3, 1 Chronicles 29:19 2 Chronicles 15:17, Chronicles 16:19; 19:9, Job 1:1, 1:8, Job2:3, Job 8:20, Job 9:21-22, 22:3, Psalm 18:32, 37:37; 101:2; 101:6, Prov. 2:21, Proverbs 4: 18. Matthew 19:21, Luke 1:3, Isaiah 1:16-17, Isaiah 26:3, Isaiah 38:3, 6:40, Romans 6:11-12, 8: 8-9, 2 Corinthians 13:11, Galatians 2:20, Philippians 3:15, 4:13, Colossians 1:28, 4:12, 2 Timothy 2:19, 3:17, Hebrew 10: 1, 13:21, James 1:4, 3:2. 1 Peter 5:10, 1 John 2:3-6, 3:6, 3:9, 4:17-18, 5:4, 5:18.

www.ingramcontent.com/pod-product-compliance
Lightning Source LLC
Chambersburg PA
CBHW062155100526
44589CB00014B/1847